Classical Themes for All Keyboards.

Wise Publications
London/New York/Sydney

Exclusive Distributors:
Music Sales Limited
8/9 Frith Street, London W1V 5TZ, England.
Music Sales Corporation
225 Park Avenue South, New York, NY10003, USA.
Music Sales Pty Limited
120 Rothschild Avenue, Rosebery, NSW 2018, Australia.

This book © Copyright 1991 by Wise Publications
Order No.AM85317
ISBN 0-7119-2709-X

Designed by Pearce Marchbank Studio
Compiled by Peter Evans
Arranged by Daniel Scott
Music processed by Seton Music Graphics

Music Sales' complete catalogue lists thousands of
titles and is free from your local music shop, or direct from Music Sales Limited.
Please send a cheque/postal order for £1.50 for postage to:
Music Sales Limited, Newmarket Road, Bury St. Edmunds,
Suffolk IP33 3YB.

Your Guarantee of Quality
As publishers, we strive to produce every book to the highest
commercial standards.
The music has been freshly engraved and the book has been carefully
designed to minimise awkward page turns and to make
playing from it a real pleasure.
Particular care has been given to specifying acid-free, neutral sized
paper which has not been chlorine bleached but produced with
special regard for the environment. Throughout, the printing and
binding have been planned to ensure a sturdy, attractive
publication which should give years of enjoyment.
If your copy fails to meet our high standards, please inform us and
we will gladly replace it.

Printed in the United Kingdom by
Caligraving Limited, Thetford, Norfolk.

Adagio

Composed by Tommaso Albinoni (1671–1750) /arr. Giazotto.

Voice: Strings   Style: Waltz

Air from 'The Water Music'

Composed by George Frideric Handel (1685–1759)

Voice: Flute   Style: Swing

Autumn from 'The Four Seasons'

Composed by Antonio Vivaldi (1675–1741)

Voice: Harpsichord   Style: Waltz (baroque)

Ave Maria

Composed by Franz Schubert (1797–1828)

Voice: Piano   No rhythm

Alleluia from 'Exultate Jubilate'

Composed by Wolfgang Amadeus Mozart (1756–1791)

Voice: Organ   Style: Eight beat

Bridal March from 'Lohengrin'

Composed by Richard Wagner (1813–1883)

Voice: Organ   Style: March

Berceuse from 'Dolly Suite'

Composed by Gabriel Fauré (1845–1924)

Voice: Harp   Style: Eight beat

Can Can from 'Orpheus In The Underworld'

Composed by Jacques Offenbach (1819–1880)

Voice: Honky tonk piano   Style: Disco

Chanson De Matin

Composed by Edward Elgar (1857–1934)

Voice: Electric piano   Style: No rhythm

Clair De Lune

Composed by Claude Debussy (1862–1918)

Voice: Piano   Style: No rhythm

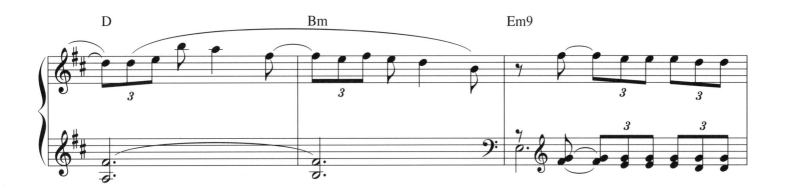

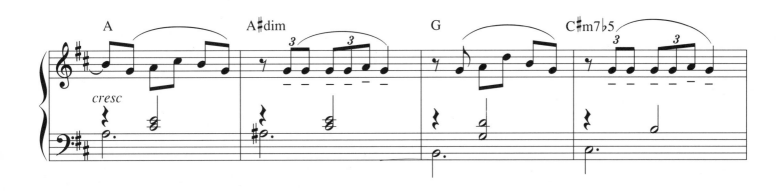

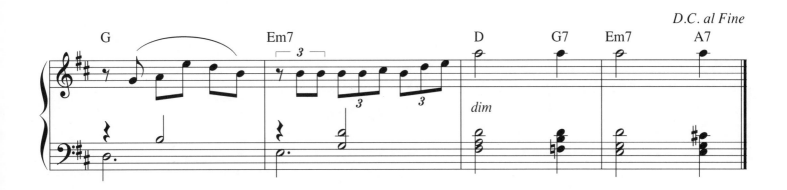

19

Theme from Clarinet Concerto

Composed by Wolfgang Amadeus Mozart (1756–1791)

Voice: Clarinet   Style: Waltz

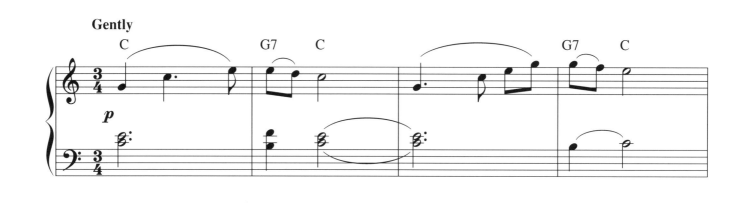

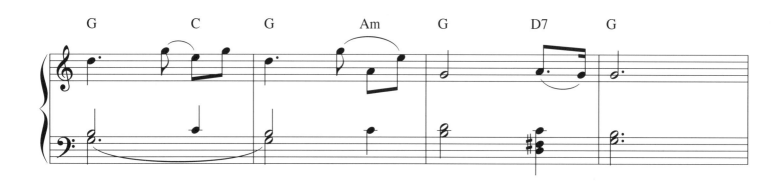

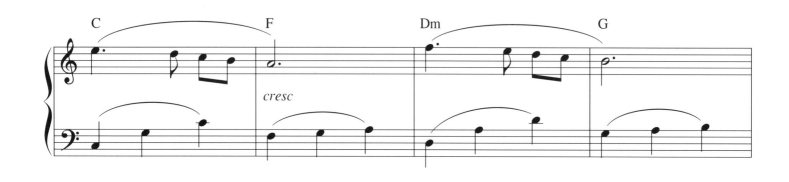

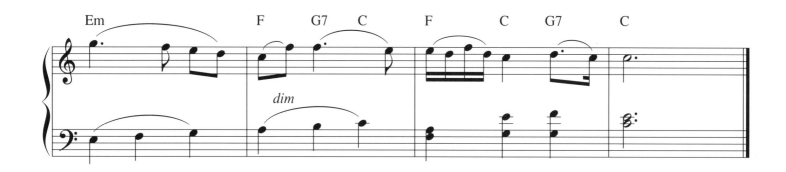

Dance Of The Hours

Composed by Amilcare Ponchielli (1834–1886)

Voice: Strings   Style: Rock

Entr'acte from 'Rosamunde'

Composed by Franz Schubert (1797–1828)

Voice: Piano   Style: Eight beat

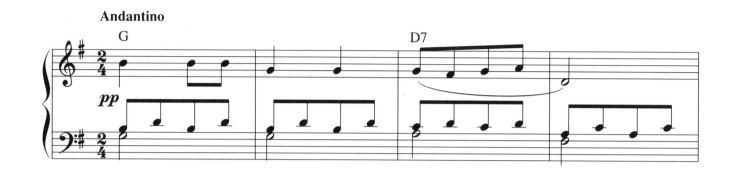

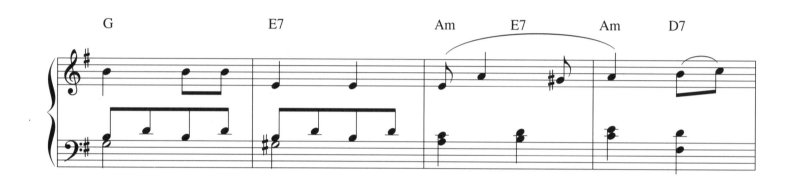

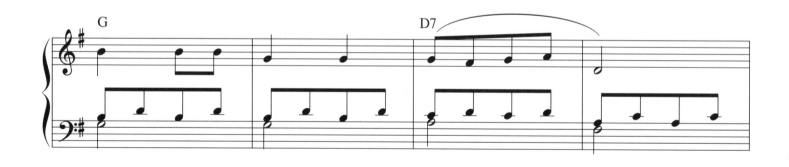

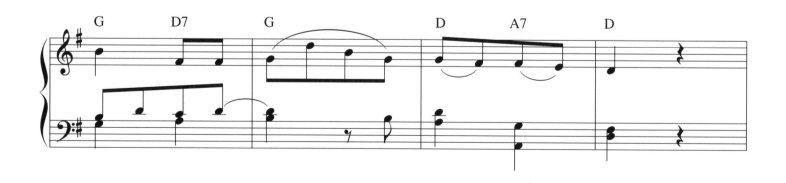

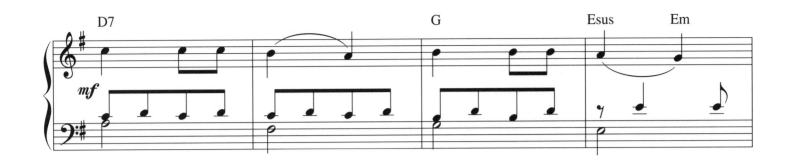

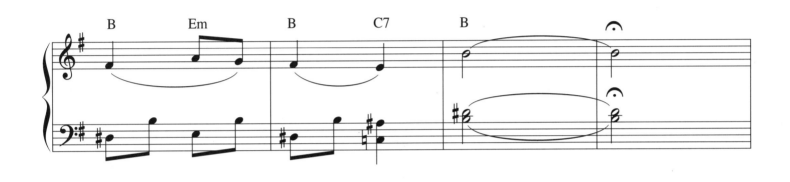

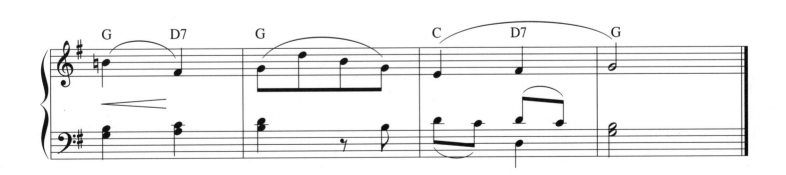

Für Elise

Composed by Ludwig van Beethoven (1770–1827)

Voice: Harp   Style: Waltz

Habanera from 'Carmen'

Composed by Georges Bizet (1838–1875)

Voice: Clarinet   Style: Habanera/Tango

The Harmonious Blacksmith

Composed by George Frideric Handel (1685–1759)

Voice: Harpsichord   Style: Eight beat

Huntsmen's Chorus

Composed by Carl Maria von Weber (1786–1826)

Voice: Bass   Style: 16 beat

I Vow To Thee My Country (Jupiter from 'The Planets')

Composed by Gustav Holst (1874–1934)

Voice: Bass   Style: Waltz

Largo

Composed by George Frideric Handel (1685–1759)

Voice: Piano   Style: Waltz

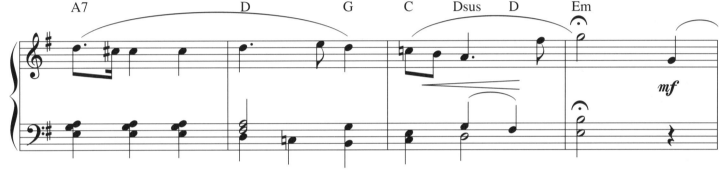

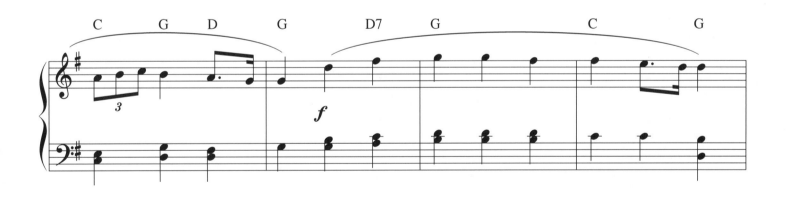

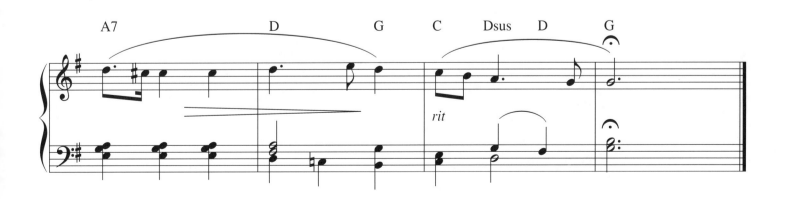

La Donna E Mobile from 'Rigoletto'

Composed by Giuseppe Verdi (1813–1901)

Voice: Strings   Style: Waltz

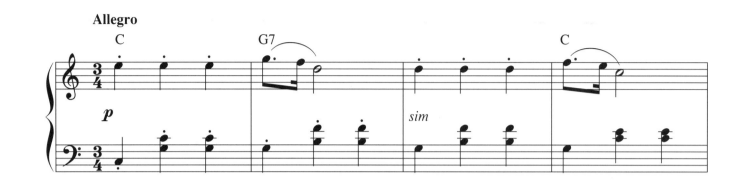

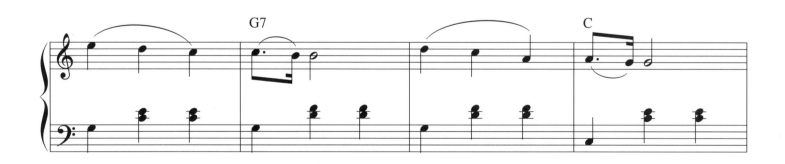

Lullaby

Composed by Johannes Brahms (1833–1897)

Voice: Piano   Style: Waltz

Minuet

Composed by Luigi Boccherini (1743–1805)

Voice: Harpsichord   Style: Waltz

Méditation from 'Thaïs'

Composed by Jules Massenet (1842–1912)

Voice: Vibes/electric piano   Style: No rhythm

Minuet In G

Composed by Johann Sebastian Bach (1685–1750)

Voice: Harpsichord   Style: Waltz

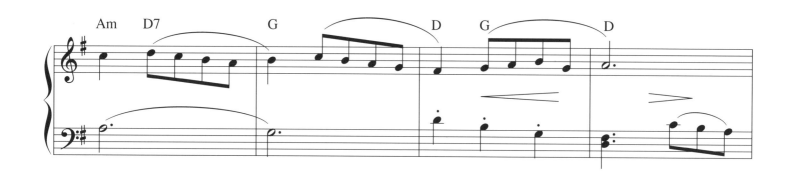

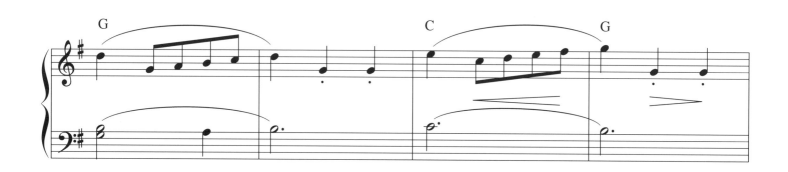

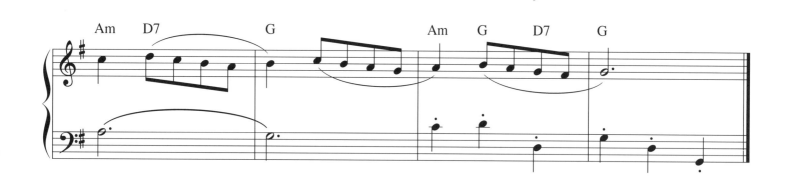

Morning from 'Peer Gynt Suite'

Composed by Edvard Grieg (1843–1907)

Voice: Flute   Style: No rhythm

Nimrod from 'Enigma Variations'

Composed by Edward Elgar (1857–1934)

Voice: Strings   Style: No rhythm

Nocturne from 'String Quartet No.2'

Composed by Alexander Borodin (1833–1887)

Voice: Strings   Style: Waltz

O, For The Wings Of A Dove

Composed by Felix Mendelssohn (1809–1847)

Voice: Piano   Style: Eight beat

O My Beloved Father from 'Gianni Schicchi'

Composed by Giacomo Puccini (1858–1924)

Voice: Strings   Style: Waltz

Ode To Joy from '9th Symphony'

Composed by Ludwig van Beethoven (1770–1827)

Voice: Bass   Style: Rock

On Wings Of Song

Composed by Felix Mendelssohn (1809–1847)

Voice: Harp   Style: Waltz

One Fine Day from 'Madam Butterfly'

Composed by Giacomo Puccini (1858–1924)

Voice: Strings   Style: Waltz

Pavane

Composed by Gabriel Fauré (1845–1924)

Voice: Flute   Style: Eight beat

Theme from Piano Concerto No.2

Composed by Wolfgang Amadeus Mozart (1756–1791)

Voice: Piano   Style: Eight beat

Theme from 'Polovtsian Dances'

Composed by Alexander Borodin (1833–1887)

Voice: Strings/electric piano   Style: Eight beat

Pilgrims' Chorus from 'Tannhäuser'

Composed by Richard Wagner (1813–1883)

Voice: Brass   Style: Waltz

Theme from Pomp & Circumstance March No.1
(Land Of Hope And Glory)

Composed by Edward Elgar (1857–1934)

Voice: Organ   Style: March

Prelude Op.28 No.7

Composed by Frédéric Chopin (1810–1849)

Voice: Piano   Style: Waltz

Theme from 'Romeo And Juliet'

Composed by Peter Ilyich Tchaikovsky (1840–1893)

Voice: Strings   Style: Eight beat

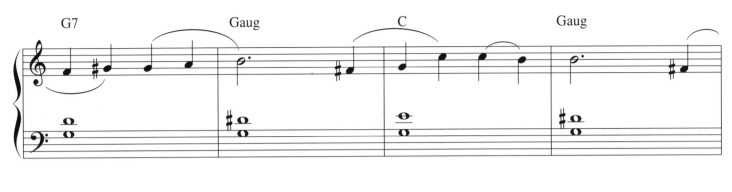

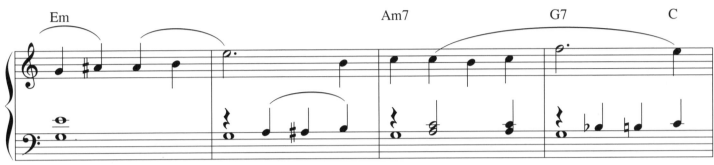

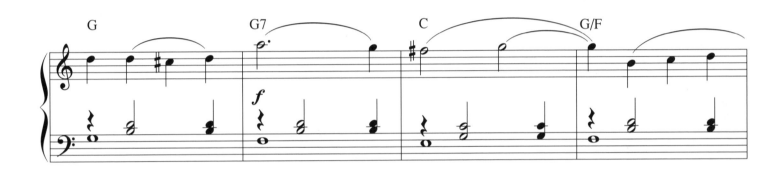

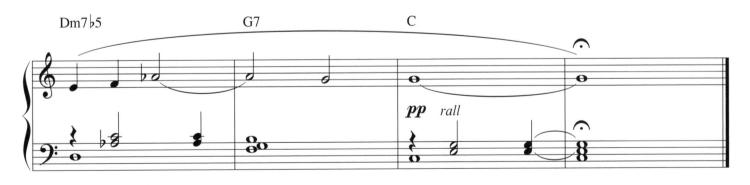

The Swan (from 'Carnival Of The Animals')

Composed by Camille Saint-Saëns (1835–1921)

Voice: Strings   Style: Waltz

Waltz from 'Swan Lake'

Composed by Peter Ilyich Tchaikovsky (1840–1893)

Voice: Strings   Style: Waltz

Tempo di valse

Sarabande from 'Suite XI'

Composed by George Frideric Handel (1685–1759)

Voice: Bass   Style: Medieval ¾

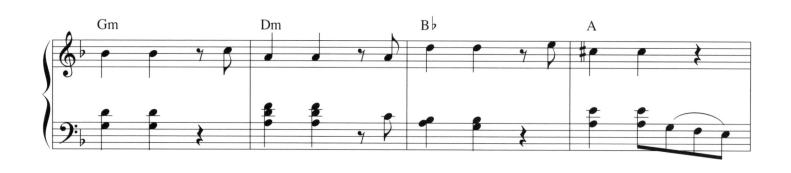

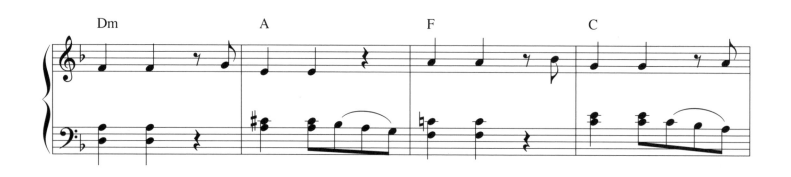

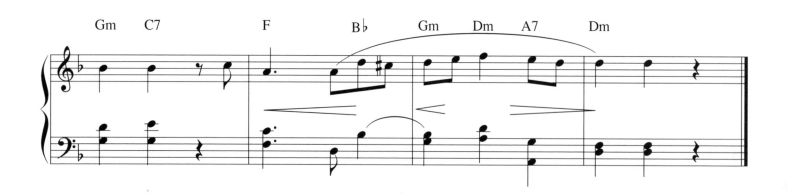

The Blue Danube

Composed by Johann Strauss II (1825–1899)

Voice: Strings/piano   Style: Waltz

Theme: 'From the New World' Symphony

Composed by Antonín Dvořák (1841–1904)

Voice: Oboe/strings   Style: No rhythm

Trumpet Tune

Composed by Jeremiah Clarke (1673 or 74–1707)

Voice: Trumpet   Style: Rock 'n' roll $\frac{12}{8}$

Trumpet Voluntary

Composed by Jeremiah Clarke (1673 or 74–1707)

Voice: Trumpet   Style: Rock

Theme from 'Variations On A Theme By Haydn' (St. Anthony Chorale)

Composed by Johannes Brahms (1833–1897)

Voice: Clarinet   Style: Eight beat

Wedding March from 'A Midsummer Night's Dream'

Composed by Felix Mendelssohn (1809–1847)

Voice: Organ   Style: March

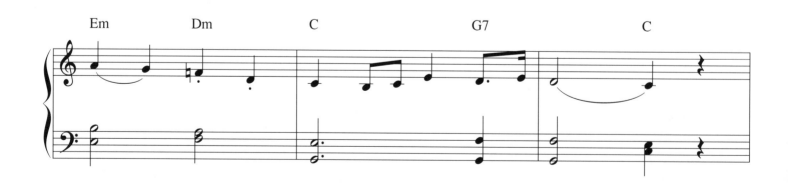

Theme from 'William Tell Overture'

Composed by Gioacchino Rossini (1792–1868)

Voice: Trumpet   Style: Disco

Waltz from 'Coppélia'

Composed by Léo Delibes (1836–1891)

Voice: Strings   Style: Waltz

7/01 (40723)